My STORY

Joseph

My life in Egypt!

Written by Fiona Boon

Illustrated by Nadine Wickenden

I0892082

My STORY

Hi there, I'm Joseph.
Let me **tell** you about the **people** in **my** story.

This is **me**,
just a **normal boy**.
My dad just **gave** me
a **brand-new** coat!

This is Pharaoh (fare-oh). He **rules** Egypt. He has a **cupbearer** to make sure his **wine** isn't poisoned!

This is my family. I have eleven **brothers**. **Reuben** is the **oldest** and **Benjamin** is the **youngest**.

This is Egypt, a very **rich** and **powerful** land.

One day, Dad **gave** me an **awesome** coat.

He had **made** it **especially** for me! I ran to **show** it to my **brothers**, but they were **really** jealous. **None** of them had a **coat** like that, so they HATED me for it.

A **few weeks** later, my **brothers** led the **sheep** away to **feed**. **Dad** sent me to **find** them and **check** on the **sheep**. When I **saw** my **brothers** in the **distance**, I gave a **big wave**, but they **ignored** me. When I **reached** them, I was **about** to say **hi**, but they **seized** me and **THREW** me in a **deep pit**.

SQUEAK!

It **felt** like I was there for HOURS, **listening** to my **brothers arguing**. All of a sudden, there was the **noise** of camels, and my **brothers** pulled me out of the **pit**.

My hands were **tied**, and the **next** thing I **knew**, I was on my way to **Egypt**. I had been **sold** as a SLAVE!

"Life **can't** get much worse than **this**," I thought, but then it did, because I was **thrown** into prison. I **couldn't** believe it!

"**One day** at a time!" I thought. "Somehow, GOD will **help me**."

And He **did**. In **prison**, I met Pharaoh's **baker** and **cupbearer**. They **both** had DREAMS, and **God** helped me **explain** them! Their **dreams showed** what would happen to them.

The **baker's** **dream** made me **sad**.
I had to **tell** him that **Pharaoh**
was **not** going to let him go **free**.

But the cupbearer **dreamed** that he **squeezed** grapes for **Pharaoh**. "**You** will be **back** serving **Pharaoh** very SOON!" I said.

Two years later, Pharaoh himself had a dream, and **no one** knew what it **meant**. The **cupbearer** told Pharaoh about **me** and they SENT for me **right away**!

"I **dreamed** I was at the Nile and seven **fat** cows came along," said **Pharaoh**. "Then seven **thin cows** ATE the fat ones. What does it **mean**? **None** of my magicians can **tell** me."

"God has **shown** you the FUTURE!" I said. "The seven **fat cows** are **seven years** when we will have **lots** of food. The **thin cows** are the **seven years** after that. **Store** food now, so **Egypt** will not starve."

Pharaoh was **so** pleased, he **decided** to **put** me in **charge** over all of **Egypt**. For **seven years** I **saved** food, so when the seven years came when **nothing** grew and many **animals** died, the people of **Egypt** did **not** go **hungry**!

FOOD STORES

One day, as I was **giving** food out to the **people**, my own brothers **arrived**! They didn't recognize me at **first**, but when I **finally** told them who I was, they **praised** God for **keeping** me SAFE all this **time**.

I brought my **whole family** back to Egypt and we lived there **together** for **many years**.

My Sticker Journal

Can you remember my story? Use the **stickers** to complete my journal.

Sticker the missing parts of my coat.

Give my coat bright colors!

My **dad gave** me an amazing **new coat**.

My **brothers** sold me as a **slave**!

Sticker the missing parts of Pharaoh's dream.

I was **taken** to Egypt.

Sticker the pyramids.

Pharaoh had a strange **dream** about the **future**!

I **told** Pharoah to start saving **food!**

Sticker some of the food I stored!

When my brothers arrived, they didn't recognize me!

Sticker my special Egyptian clothes!

Sticker my family's new homes!

I **missed** my family, so they came to **live** in **Egypt** with me.